Goats

Kate Riggs

CREATIVE EDUCATION • CREATIVE PAPERBACKS

Published by Creative Education and Creative Paperbacks
P.O. Box 227, Mankato, Minnesota 56002
Creative Education and Creative Paperbacks
are imprints of The Creative Company
www.thecreativecompany.us

Design by Ellen Huber; production by Joe Kahnke
Art direction by Rita Marshall
Printed in the United States of America

Photographs by Alamy (Lena Ason, Joye Ardyn Durham, Lori
Eanes, Juniors Bildarchiv GmbH, Manfred Ruckszio, Sarawut
Suksao), Dreamstime (Norma Cornes, Eovsyannikova, Iakov
Filimonov, Isselee, Ksena2009, Dmytro Lypchak, Sa83lim,
Komprach Sapanrat, Tanyaru, Zelli), iStockphoto (Juanmonino,
LazingBee), Shutterstock (AsyaPozniak, Gherzak, successo images)

Library of Congress Cataloging-in-Publication Data
Riggs, Kate.
Goats / Kate Riggs.
p. cm. — (Seedlings)
Includes bibliographical references and index.
Summary: A kindergarten-level introduction to goats,
covering their growth process, behaviors, the farms they call
home, and such defining features as their horns.
ISBN 978-1-60818-785-0 (hardcover)
ISBN 978-1-62832-393-1 (pbk)
ISBN 978-1-56660-827-5 (eBook)
This title has been submitted for
CIP processing under LCCN 2016937130.

CCSS: RI.K.1, 2, 3, 4, 5, 6, 7;
RI.1.1, 2, 3, 4, 5, 6, 7; RF.K.1, 3; RF.1.1

First Edition HC 9 8 7 6 5 4 3 2 1
First Edition PBK 9 8 7 6 5 4 3 2 1

TABLE OF CONTENTS

Hello, goats!

Some goats are
farm animals.
Other goats
are wild.

Groups of goats are kept on pastures.

Hairy goats are many colors. They have white, brown, gray, or black hair.

Some goats have spots or stripes of color.

Goat tails are short and point up.

Goat hooves have two toes.
Most goats have two horns.

Goats eat many
things. They eat
grasses and weeds.

They eat woody plants and leaves.

Baby goats are called kids. They drink milk at first. Then they start eating plants.

Curious **goats climb everything.**

They try to
get out of a
pen or fence.

Goodbye, goats!

Picture a Goat

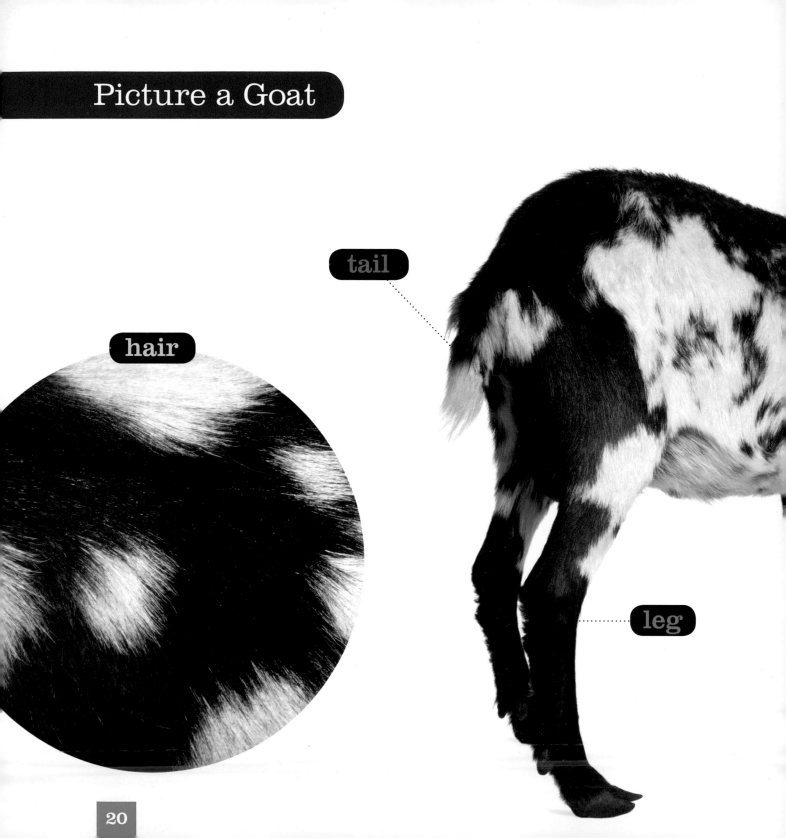

hair

tail

leg

horns

eye

nose

beard

hoof

curious: wanting to know more about something

hooves: horny parts of goats' feet

pastures: lands covered with grass and other plants

Read More

Green, Emily K. *Goats*.
Minneapolis: Bellwether Media, 2007.

Meister, Cari. *Goats*.
Minneapolis: Jump!, 2013.

Websites

Activity Village: Goat Crafts
http://www.activityvillage.co.uk/goat-crafts
Use paper plates and other materials to make your own goats.

DLTK's Goat Coloring Pages
http://www.coloring.ws/goat.htm
Print out a picture of a goat to color.

Index